New Evangelization

✠

Passing on the Catholic Faith Today

✠

CARDINAL DONALD WUERL

OUR SUNDAY VISITOR PUBLISHING DIVISION
OUR SUNDAY VISITOR, INC.
HUNTINGTON, INDIANA 46750

ISBN: 978-1-61278-698-8 (Inventory No. T1403)
eISBN: 978-1-61278-302-4
LCCN: 2012955315

Cover design: Lindsey Riesen
Interior design: Dianne Nelson

PRINTED IN THE UNITED STATES OF AMERICA

New
Evangelization

CONTENTS

Summaries and Reflections for
Personal and Parish Use

At the end of each chapter, you will find summaries and reflections which are designed for personal use or group discussion. They are intended especially for pastors and adult formation directors who wish to study this text and the New Evangelization in parish programs. Ideal for small groups, answers to the reflection questions could be written and/or discussed at the parish level. Individual readers would also welcome these additions as they help mediate the message and mission of the New Evangelization for personal faith development. The boxed sections are taken directly from the text and will help to highlight a strong point in each chapter.

PREFACE

A s I took my aisle seat on the plane, the woman in the window seat turned and introduced herself, and seeing my Roman collar she said, "Have you been born again?" "Yes," I responded, and she immediately asked, "When?"

I said: "In baptism. And I have been trying to grow into that new life ever since." "Oh," she said, "you're Catholic," which led her to another question and the beginning of a conversation that lasted the entire flight. She noted that as Catholics we are "big on this Church thing." She recognized this was a major difference between us. Then, she showed me her small prayer book that had in it a number of quotations from the New Testament reminding us that we have received new life in Christ and asked, "Tell me about this Church thing that is so important to you."

We began with Matthew's Gospel and Peter's confession about Jesus that led to Jesus' announcement, "You are Peter, and upon this rock I will build my church" (Mt 16:18).

As the conversation unfolded, and as she raised a number of significant questions, we talked about Jesus establishing his new Body, the Church, how we are all invited into the family of God, how the apostles' mission continues today through the bishops who lead the Church, and how the work of Saint Peter is carried on today by the Bishop of Rome, the pope.

As we landed and were taxiing up to the gate, the man in the aisle seat directly across from me leaned over and said: "Father, I couldn't help but hear this conversation. I'm Catholic, and I didn't know all of that."

Those conversations recalled for me a still earlier conversation I had on a flight going to one of our bishops' conference meetings. As I took my seat, the man in the seat next to me asked where I was going. With a smile, I answered, "To the same destination you are, I hope!" He chuckled and added, "No, what I meant to say was, 'What's the purpose of your trip?'" I told him and then asked him why he was traveling. Sounding discouraged, he said, "I'm going to the first Communion of my kid brother's kid." Then to add emphasis to his displeasure, he said, "I'm going because my mother called and said, 'I want to see you there.'"

I interjected that a first Communion is a very happy event. He shot back, "Maybe for you." This unfolded into a two-hour-long conversation about holy Communion, the Mass and the Eucharist. My travel companion claimed to be Catholic, or, as he described it, "a Catholic who is no longer into the faith." The more we talked, the more it was clear he had no real understanding of what the Catholic faith teaches on something as basic as the Eucharist. He said he had been to some religious education programs when he was little, but that they had not meant much to him.

This time around, though, he showed real interest in what he thought he already knew. He was now realizing he was mistaken or simply missing information about the faith of the Church.

As our plane landed and taxied up to the gate, he turned and very seriously said, "Thanks, Father, for talking to me about this Eucharist thing; it's really cool," and then corrected himself, "I mean really great."

During the recent Synod on the New Evangelization, those conversations came flooding back. In one way or another, they represented all the different manifestations of why we need a New Evangelization and to whom, in one way or another, it should be directed.

The New Evangelization will likely resonate with so many of our young people who are actively searching for a deeper connectedness to the Church. The night before I left Washington for the synod meeting in Rome, I had Mass with a large number of students who are part of the campus ministry program at George Washington University. Following the Mass, I joined the chaplain and the students for some burritos. The students were happy to tell me that under the direction and encouragement of their energetic chaplain, they think of themselves as apostles on the campus, charged to bring somebody else back to Mass.

Only a short time before, I had met with a number of students at The Catholic University of America who were also very much committed to coming together in small groups to deepen their prayer life and their understanding of the faith.

Almost immediately after I returned from the synod, I visited the Catholic Center at the University of Maryland, where I celebrated Mass for several hundred students and then joined them for a buffet supper. The students were quick to point out to me how their chaplain, who concelebrated Mass with me and whom they greatly appreciated, continually urges them to invite fellow students to Mass. Next to me at the supper was a young lady in the RCIA (Rite of Christian Initiaion of Adults) program who told me that it was precisely because of an invitation she had received to come to Mass that she eventually came to the decision to become a member of the Church.

Still another example of the New Evangelization now at work is the presence of councils of the Knights of Columbus on both secular and Catholic campuses throughout the Archdiocese of Washington.

In this reflection, I want to explore the New Evangelization and what it means for the Church — for all of us — today. To do this, we will need to look briefly at what a synod is, and then the fruit of its work. It seems most appropriate since the recent Synod on the New Evangelization is the first concerted effort on the part of the Church to address, at one time, the many elements of the New Evangelization.

INTRODUCTION

A synod is a gathering of bishops who are representative of the Church throughout the entire world. The pope convokes such a meeting, and conferences of bishops around the world elect those bishops who will attend. The pope also appoints a certain number of additional bishops, experts, and observers. The Synod for the New Evangelization for the Transmission of the Christian Faith called by Pope Benedict XVI convened October 7-28, 2012.

In response to the pope's invitation, more than 250 bishops from around the world gathered in Rome. They were joined by nearly 100 men and women representatives of the Church, including many from religious communities, and others involved in work related to evangelization.

If I had to choose three words to describe the outcome of the synod, or at least the mood of the synod, I would say that the synod was a "positive" experience, an expression of "unity," and clearly "pastoral" in its orientation.

The Church has passed through a period of great upheaval, and even in some places disorientation, in the decades of the 1970s, '80s, and even part of the '90s. But we are in a new moment in the life of the Church and are moving in the right direction.

At the Basilica of Saint Paul Outside the Walls in Rome, on the eve of the feast of the Great Apostles of Rome, Saints Peter and Paul, June 28, 2012, Pope Benedict summoned the entire Church to the timely and timeless task of the New Evangelization. That evening, the pope announced he was going to create a pontifical council whose principal task is to promote the New Evangelization. We are called, in the words of our Holy Father, "to re-propose the perennial truth of Christ's Gospel" (Homily, June 28, 2012).

The Synod on the New Evangelization concluded with a list of fifty-eight propositions. These are statements of varying length, each focused on one aspect of the three-week discussion of the members of the synod. Given the significance of the propositions, I will try to weave them into these reflections on the New Evangelization, what it means, and how it takes place in the life of the Church today.

In the last days of the synod and my stay in Rome, I was asked by a number of groups to discuss with them the work and particularly my appreciation of the outcome of the synod. One group, led by Curtis Martin, the head of FOCUS (Fellowship of Catholic University Students), consisted of representatives of FOCUS from around the United States. Another group was made up of Canadian lay evangelizers, called Catholic Christian Outreach, many of whom also work on campuses.

I pointed out to those groups and to others that what struck me about this particular synod was the unity of the bishops. We were only a few days into the working sessions when it was very clear that all of the bishops present shared a profound unity when it came to the principles of the faith, the pastoral implementation of our faith, and the need for the New Evangelization.

CHAPTER 1

✠

Evangelization and the New Evangelization

At the Mass on Sunday, October 28, at Saint Peter's Basilica for the closing of the synod, Pope Benedict XVI reflected on some aspects of the New Evangelization. He spoke of the three areas and dimensions of sharing and living the Gospel. The New Evangelization, he said, "applies, in the first instance, to the ordinary pastoral ministry that must be more animated by the fire of the Spirit." We shall return to this point when we look at all of the ways in which we can be engaged in our own parish life, in renewing our faith and helping to fan into flame the embers of the Holy Spirit that animate the Church.

The second aspect of the New Evangelization, the pope pointed out, is the Church's task "to evangelize, to proclaim the message of salvation to those who do not know Jesus Christ." This we traditionally refer to as the *missio ad gentes*, or "mission to the nations." We all recall the terms "foreign missions" and "mission lands." During the synod, it was emphasized, the pope went on to say, that there were still many regions "whose inhabitants await with lively expectation, sometimes without being fully aware of it, the first proclamation of the Gospel." The essential missionary work continues as it always has.

Sacred Scripture provides us with a clear indication of the intense commitment of the infant Church to missionary activity. There was urgency about the need to spread the Gospel, as well as awareness that the missionary activity and identity of the Church are intimately linked. Even a cursory glance at the Acts of the Apostles reveals a self-understanding on the part of the apostles that the fledgling Church was missionary by its very nature. The apostles were witnesses of the Resurrection and our salvation in and through Christ. The spread and acceptance of the message marked the growth of the Church.

The third aspect, the pope noted in his homily, concerns "the baptized whose lives do not reflect the demands of baptism ... the Church is particularly concerned that they should encounter Jesus Christ anew, rediscover the joy of faith. and return to religious practice in the community of the faithful."

This last point, the re-proposing of the Good News to those who have drifted away from the faith, we will look at in more detail. The pope's homily was also reflected in one of the propositions approved by all of the synodal fathers. It should be noted that of the fifty-eight propositions, all of them received nearly unanimous approbation.

In Proposition 7, we read: "Evangelization can be understood in three aspects. First, evangelization *ad gentes* is the announcement of the Gospel to those who do not know Jesus Christ. Secondly, it also includes the continuing growth in faith that is the ordinary life of the Church. Finally, the New Evangelization is directed especially to those who have become distant from the Church" (Prop. 7: New Evangelization as a Permanent Missionary Dimension of the Church).

It is increasingly clear that the New Evangelization is not one specific action or activity of the Church, but rather a way of seeing a whole range of activities carried on by the Church to spread the Good News of Jesus Christ. Thus we can speak about the ongoing outreach to those who have never heard of Jesus. At the same time, it means a continuity with the ongoing catechesis that is a part of the life of every believer. Finally, it involves outreach to those who have simply fallen away from the practice of the faith.

ALL EVANGELIZATION BEGINS WITH JESUS CHRIST

The embrace in the love of Jesus and the joy of his Gospel of new life are meant to be savored, cherished, and shared. New Evangelization, as does all evangelization, begins with the experience of Jesus Christ.

Everything the Church is, she has received from Christ. The first and most precious of his gifts is the grace bestowed through the Paschal Mystery: his passion, death and glorious resurrection. Jesus has freed us from the power of sin and saved us from death. The Church receives from her Lord not only the tremendous grace he has won for us, but also the commission to share and to make known his victory. We are summoned to transmit faithfully the Gospel of Jesus Christ to the world. The Church's primary mission is evangelization.

The word "evangelization" comes from the Greek word for "Gospel," ευαγγέλιον, or *evangelium*. The Gospel is the announcement of the "good message," or "Good News," that Jesus is God's Son and our Savior.

The Church never tires of announcing the gift she has received from the Lord. The Second Vatican Council has reminded us that evangelization is at the very heart of the Church. In *Lumen Gentium* (*Dogmatic Constitution on the Church*), the fundamental text and nucleus of the council's expression on the life of the Church, the council fathers emphasized, "The Church has received this solemn mandate of Christ to proclaim the saving truth from the apostles and must carry it out to the very ends of the earth" (17). The council spoke eloquently of the truth that the divine mission that Jesus entrusted to the Church continues through the apostles and their successors, and will last until the end of the world.

The duty to proclaim the saving truth is not just the responsibility of clergy and religious. On the contrary, the council stressed the important role of "every disciple of Christ" in the mission of "spreading the faith." The council fathers accentuated the crucial and vital participation of every Catholic, especially through the eager dedication and gifts of the lay faithful to the mission of evangelization: "The laity go forth as powerful proclaimers ... when they courageously join to their profession of faith a life springing from faith. This evangelization, that is, this announcing of Christ by a living testimony as well as by the spoken word, takes on a specific quality and a special force in that it is carried out in the ordinary surroundings of the world" (*LG*, 35).

In his apostolic exhortation *Evangelii nuntiandi* (*On Evangelization in the Modern World*), Pope Paul VI drew on the teaching of the council when he affirmed that the Church is "a community which is in its turn evangelizing. The command to the Twelve to go out and proclaim the Good News is also valid for all Christians, though in a different way ... the Good News of the kingdom which is coming and which has begun is meant for all people of all times. Those who have received the Good News and who have been gathered by it into the community of salvation can and must communicate and spread it" (13). In this historic document, issued ten years to the day of the close of the Second Vatican Council, Pope Paul VI discerned the need for "a new period of evangelization."

"New in Ardor, Methods, and Expression"

Blessed John Paul II reminded us that evangelization is "the primary service which the Church can render to every individual and to all humanity," and he took up the commitment begun by Pope Paul VI to an evangelization "new in ardor, methods, and expression."

Blessed John Paul II can rightfully be considered the father of the New Evangelization. For over twenty-six years he exercised a worldwide ministry that was rooted in the understanding that his task was to be supreme pastor of the Church. He was to feed his sheep, to be the rock upon which the Church rests, to sustain and strengthen the faith of us all. This message he carried to the ends of the earth in visits to every continent and to nearly every nation. He spoke a multiplicity of languages in an unending sequence of events. He used his office to proclaim the Church's teaching in a way that awakened a desire for renewal of the faith in the hearts of thousands and thousands of people. He was not only the voice of the New Evangelization; he was its principal apostle. We are told that in his long and extraordinary ministry, he visited over 130 countries, traveling more than 750,000 miles to meet his flock across the face of the planet.

Pope Benedict XVI has focused the mission of the Church Universal on the task of the New Evangelization. I found it particularly interesting that, as the synod was closing, Pope Benedict announced that he was consolidating the work of the New Evangelization and catechesis in the Pontifical Council for the New Evangelization. The Congregation for the Clergy had previously overseen the work of catechesis. Our own bishops' conference, in its reorganization a few years ago, did something along the same lines by creating a

Committee on Evangelization and Catechesis. All of these structural reorganizations are meant to highlight the continuity between and the overlapping of efforts of evangelization, catechesis, and outreach to those who have already been baptized.

The synod made it very clear that the continuation of the mission of Christ, which began with the Great Commissioning following his death and resurrection, is what we are engaged in today. As the Acts of the Apostles tells us, as Jesus prepared to return to his Father in glory, he charged his disciples, "You will be my witnesses" (Acts 1:8). That same challenge echoes in our ears and hearts today — we are the witnesses to Jesus Christ, his message, his way of life, his triumph over death, and his pledge of new life to all who would walk with him.

The United States Conference of Catholic Bishops some time ago developed a vision of evangelization into a plan and strategy called *Go and Make Disciples*. Today the conference's Committee on Evangelization and Catechesis is working to focus the efforts of the Church in our country on the New Evangelization, centered on a renewal of the faith that brings with it fresh confidence and, therefore, a willingness to reach out to others and share the great gift of the Gospel.

Evangelization and the New Evangelization

The New Evangelization is not one specific action or activity of the Church, but rather a way of seeing a whole range of activities carried on by the Church to spread the Good News of Jesus Christ.

SUMMARY

Pope Benedict XVI has highlighted three aspects of the New Evangelization — that is, the sharing and living of the Gospel of Jesus Christ in today's world. First, the pope reminds us that our "ordinary pastoral ministry must be more animated by the fire of the Spirit." Second, we are called to proclaim the Gospel to those people "who do not know Jesus Christ." Finally, the mission of the New Evangelization is to find new ways to help renew the faith lives of people who have drifted away from the Church so that they may "encounter Jesus Christ anew, rediscover the joy of faith and return to the religious practice in the community of faithful."

FOR REFLECTION

What are some ways you proclaim the Good News of Jesus Christ in your daily life? How might we encourage and welcome friends and family back into the Church? Do you take the time to listen to the leadings of the Holy Spirit?

CHAPTER 2

✠

The Context Today
of Our Faith Proclamation

The New Evangelization responds to a real and urgent need in the Church today. The context of our faith proclamation is the highly secular view of life in our culture that bleaches out recognition and appreciation of God and religious faith.

Some time ago, I was given a copy of what is referred to as the "Jefferson Bible." The third president of the United States, Thomas Jefferson, assembled a book that he entitled, "The Life and Morals of Jesus of Nazareth." In it, he arranges a chronology and edited story of Jesus's life, parables, and moral teachings while eliminating any reference to supernatural events, the divinity of Christ and his miracles, particularly, the Resurrection. The result was an extremely limited view of Jesus that missed the truly significant part of who he is and what he accomplished. I think of that volume when I reflect on our culture today. It does not seem prepared to look beyond a very limited horizon that excludes God, religious faith, and the wonder of the spiritual dimension of human life.

In my opening address at the synod, I attempted to sum up what so many conferences of bishops from around the world indicated as the number one challenge of the day — secularism. This limited view of life has resulted in a dramatically changing societal background for the reception, appropriation, and living of the faith. This reality is the context of our proclamation of the Gospel — our bearing witness to Jesus Christ today.

Across the Church, we deal in many instances, but particularly in most of the so-called First World countries, with a dramatic reduction in the practice of the faith among those who are already baptized. The responses from bishops in the so-called Third World — more recently evangelized societies — indicate the same experience in their own local churches.

OUR SECULARIZED CULTURE

Secularization has fashioned two generations of Catholics who do not know the Church's foundational prayers. Many do not sense a value in Mass attendance. They fail to receive the Sacrament of Penance, and have often lost a sense of mystery or the transcendent as having any real and verifiable meaning.

As we undertake the New Evangelization and the presentation of the richness of the experience of Jesus and his Gospel, we must be aware of the context in which this arduous task unfolds. The context of the New Evangelization and the very reason why we need to re-propose our Catholic faith to our world, is the secularism that is now rapidly enveloping our society and Western culture.

The New Evangelization recognizes that in countries where the Gospel has already been preached there is an "eclipse of the sense of God" (*Evangelium vitae*, 21). What brings a new urgency to our mission is the acknowledgment of just how widespread and profound is the new secularism.

In the beginning of our work at the synod, we were greatly aided by the reflections from bishops representing five continents who spoke to us of challenges and, at the same time, of the communion of the Church. All of the interventions expressed aspects of the actual situation that we find in the Church around the world.

For example, Cardinal Péter Erdő, the archbishop of Esztergom-Budapest, in Hungary, president of the Hungarian Episcopal Conference, and president of the Council of European Episcopal Conferences, stated very clearly: "Europe must be evangelized. It needs it.... De-Christianization is accompanied by repeated juridical as well as physical attacks against the visible presence of the manifestations of faith."

Cardinal Polycarp Pengo, the archbishop of Dar-es-Salaam, in Tanzania, and the president of the Symposium of Episcopal Conferences of Africa and Madagascar, also noted that "globalization introduces rapidly undigested foreign values, making it hard for Christians on the continent to be truly Africans. Their Christian faith is thus rendered also very much alien."

Speaking on behalf of the Episcopal Conference of Mexico and the Latin American Episcopal Council, Archbishop Carlos Aguiar Retes of Mexico reminded the synod that "the pastoral of the Church cannot ignore the historical context in which its members live. It lives in very concrete social, cultural contexts. These social and cultural transformations represent naturally new challenges for the Church in its mission of building the kingdom of God."

The archbishop of Mumbai, India, and general secretary of the Federation of Asian Bishops' Conferences, Cardinal Oswald Gracias, noted: "An overarching megatrend that impacts every aspect of Asian life is globalization. This is an ongoing, inexorable, complex, and ambivalent process which impacts every sphere of life and activity.... The effects of globalization are seen overall affecting our value systems. Traditional Asian values, much-cherished traditions, and cultures are being impacted and eroded."

And, finally, speaking as president of the New Zealand Episcopal Conference and president of the Federation of Catholic Bishops Conferences of Oceania, Archbishop John Dew, of Wellington, New Zealand, noted, "We need to reclaim the Catholic kerygmatic tradition 'to speak the Word of God boldly — in season and out of season,' to reclaim the prophetic voice of the Church, to discern the signs of the times that call for the New Evangelization, and to engage in proclaiming and living a Christian response to these signs of the times."

Even as they were diverse in particulars, all of the continents manifested a need for the New Evangelization insofar as the process of secularization affects their own cultures, even though it is displayed differently in various geographic areas.

The first evangelization of Europe and America took place over several centuries. Members of religious communities and local clergy traveled long distances and visited vast territories bringing the Word and sacraments to early settlers who were deeply devoted to living the faith of their ancestors in a new land.

As growth continued, more and more dioceses were established. Local parishes maintained regular patterns of worship and devotional practices, built up faith communities, and provided religious instruction. The Catholic parish in the local neighborhood became the center of social life for Catholics and provided an immediate venue for passing on the faith. In a society which often looked on Catholics with suspicion and prejudice, the parish was particularly attuned to missionary outreach to those who had immigrated to America.

The system of Catholic education based on the local Catholic school became an extensive and formidable network for evangelization and catechesis. However, dedicated religious women and men who staffed the school as sisters, brothers, and priests were more numerous than today.

Societal standards and institutions affirmed and supported marriage and the family, providing a stable and predictable home life. The pace of life allowed for the gradual faith formation so vital to the development and sustenance of Catholic identity.

But times change. Contemporary culture has reached a point where it turns off what is not immediately accessible. Our society prefers to listen in sound bites, rather than in semesters. Slogans replace thoughtful explanations. The broad advances of globalization and social media over a relatively short span of time have had significant effects on daily life. The Church has experienced a considerable decline in the number of priests and religious. The significance of neighborhood and local relationships seem less important to a highly mobile society.

In speaking at the synod about the circumstances of our day, I pointed out that entire generations have become disassociated from the support systems that facilitated the transmission of the faith. It is as if a tsunami of secular influence has swept across the cultural landscape, taking with it such societal markers as marriage, family, the concept of the common good, and objective definitions of right and wrong.

Barriers to the Gospel

Living out a life of faith today and attempting to share the excitement of our experience of the Lord brings us into contact with many obstacles and barriers. Pope Benedict XVI, during his visit to the Archdiocese of Washington in

April 2008, underlined three challenges the Gospel faces in our society. In his homily at vespers with the bishops of the United States during a meeting at the Basilica of the National Shrine of the Immaculate Conception, he reminded us that we are challenged by secularism, the materialism around us, and the individualism that is so much a part of our culture:

> While it is true that this country is marked by a genuinely religious spirit, the subtle influence of *secularism* can nevertheless color the way people allow their faith to influence their behavior.... Any tendency to treat religion as a private matter must be resisted. Only when their faith permeates every aspect of their lives do Christians become truly open to the transforming power of the Gospel.

> For an affluent society, a further obstacle to an encounter with the living God lies in the subtle influence of *materialism*, which can all too easily focus the attention on the hundredfold, which God promises now in this time, at the expense of the eternal life which he promises in the age to come (cf. Mk 10:30).... People need to be constantly reminded to cultivate a relationship with him who came that we might have life in abundance (cf. Jn 10:10).

> In a society which values personal freedom and autonomy, it is easy to lose sight of our dependence on others as well as the responsibilities that we bear towards them. This emphasis on *individualism* has even affected the Church (cf. *Spe salvi*, 13-15), giving rise to a form of piety which sometimes emphasizes our private re-

lationship with God at the expense of our calling to be members of a redeemed community.... If this seems countercultural, that is simply further evidence of the urgent need for a renewed evangelization of culture.

The Pope diagnoses the struggles we face. The full transmission of the faith to recent generations has encountered rocks, weeds, and a soil at once hard and dry. The illusion that lurks behind many of the contemporary trends and tendencies has disrupted authentic religious experience.

Consumerism suggests that our worth is found in the things we accumulate. Individualism demands that we rely on no one but ourselves, and our personal needs always take first place. Skepticism pressures us to trust only what we can observe and measure, purports to destroy the classical and time-tested relationship between faith and reason, and threatens to reject the basic right to religious liberty and freedom of conscience.

The attempt to recast human sexuality as casual and entirely recreational has led to an untold weakening of and continued assault on marriage and family life. Autonomy convinces us that fidelity to faith only restricts us. The popular absorption with constant activity leads us to believe that unless we are always busy and life is hectic, we are behind schedule. In this setting, it becomes commonplace to treat the human person as an object to be used, and to focus almost exclusively on material gain. The swift decline in standards of entertainment has exposed our youngest children to repeated displays of intense violence. These trends coalesce and govern our every thought with a cruel relativism, and fuel ideologies that lead to a worldview of pervasive secularism.

In his apostolic letter *Tertio Millennio Adveniente* (*On the Coming of the Third Millennium*), Blessed John Paul II referred to a "crisis of civilization" and raised the question as to whether religious indifference, de-Christianization, and atheism were not found in their most widespread form in secularism.

Affirming the context of our proclamation of the Gospel today, the synod recognized this trend of secularization and called on the Christian faithful to respond. In Proposition 8, the synod wrote: "As Christians we cannot remain indifferent to the process of secularization. We are, in fact, in a situation similar to that of the first Christians and as such we should see this both as a challenge and a possibility" (Prop. 8: Witnessing in a Secularized World).

We can turn to one of the propositions to see the mind of the synod on this point. Proposition 13, which begins the section on the context of the Church's mission today, tells us, "The proclamation of the Good News in different contexts of the world — marked by the processes of globalization and secularism — places different challenges before the Church: at times in an outright religious persecution, at other times in a widespread indifference, interference, restriction, or harassment" (Prop. 13: Challenges of Our Time).

The Gospel offers us a whole new way of seeing life and the world around us. We recognize that we cannot impose this Good News of the gratuitous love of God, but at the same time do need to recognize that we are called to share this news, to bring it to others, to let them know of the beauty of life in Christ.

We bring a fuller vision — offering another dimension to life. In the Sermon on the Mount presented in Matthew's Gospel, we hear of a new way of life and how it involves the merciful, those who hunger and thirst for righteousness, those who mourn, the peacemakers, the poor in spirit. Here we learn of the call to be "salt of the earth" and a light "set on a lampstand." Later, in that same Gospel, we hear the extraordinary dictum that we should see in one another the very presence of Christ. Jesus's disciples are challenged to envision a world where not only the hungry are fed, the thirsty are given drink, the stranger is welcomed, and the naked are clothed, but also, most amazingly, sins are forgiven, and eternal life is pledged.

The Context Today of Our Faith Proclamation

Secularization has fashioned two generations of Catholics who do not know the Church's foundational prayers. Many do not sense a value in Mass attendance, fail to receive the Sacrament of Penance, and have often lost a sense of mystery or the transcendent as having any real and verifiable meaning.

SUMMARY

Our modern, globalized culture has radically changed the way the Gospel message is interpreted and understood. Secularism — the total lack of religion and belief — is rapidly enveloping our society and Western culture, leading to generations of people who do not know the foundations of the faith. Materialism (or consumerism) and individualism are also pervasive barriers to the Gospel. The New Evangelization is an effort to overcome these barriers and make the message of Jesus Christ known and loved throughout the world.

FOR REFLECTION

How do you stay true to your Catholic faith in the midst of our secular society? What are some practical ways for us to battle materialism or consumerism when they are so pervasive in our society today? Why is individualism — elevating the importance of the individual above all else — a barrier to our faith?

CHAPTER 3

✠

The Kerygma — the Core
of the Good News

Christian life is defined by an encounter with Jesus. Our proclamation is focused on Jesus, his Gospel, and his way. When Jesus first came among us, he offered a whole new way of living. The excitement spread as God's Son, who is also one of us, announced the coming of the Kingdom. The invitation to discipleship and a place in the Kingdom that he held out to those who heard him, he continues to offer today. This has been true for twenty centuries. As his message became more fully understood, it also became evident that Jesus offers us not only a new way of living but a whole new way of being. As Saint Peter wrote: "Blessed be the God and Father of our Lord Jesus Christ, who in his great mercy gave us a new birth to a living hope through the resurrection of Jesus Christ from the dead" (1 Pt 1:3). This new life as a child of God through baptism is revealed to us by Jesus himself: "Amen, amen, I say to you, no one can enter the kingdom of God without being born of water and Spirit" (Jn 3:5).

The Gospel that Jesus Christ came to reveal is not merely information about God, but rather God himself in our midst. God made himself visible, audible, tangible. In return, he asks for our love.

Among the propositions of the synod, there are several that speak to the fact that the New Evangelization is all about announcing the Good News about Jesus. For instance,

31

in Proposition 9, we read: "The foundation of all initial proclamation, the *kerygmatic* dimension, the Good News, makes
prominent an explicit announcement of salvation. 'For I de-
livered to you as of first importance what I also received, that
Christ died for our sins in accordance with the scriptures, that
he was buried, that he was raised on the third day in accordance with the scriptures, that he appeared to Cephas, then to
the twelve' (1 Cor 15:3-5).... At the same time there has to
be a continuity between the first proclamation and catechesis
which instructs us in the deposit of the faith" (Prop. 9: New
Evangelization, An Initial Proclamation).

THE HOLY TRINITY, SOURCE OF THE NEW EVANGELIZATION

The central doctrine of the Good News of the Catholic
faith is the mystery of the Holy Trinity. Proposition 4, the
first under the section titled "The Nature of the New
Evangelization," tells us that "the Church and her evangelizing mission have their origin and source in the most
Holy Trinity according to the plan of the Father, the work
of the Son, which culminated in his death and glorious
Resurrection, and the mission of the Holy Spirit. The Church
continues this mission of God's love in our world" (Prop.
4: The Holy Trinity, Source of the New Evangelization).

The importance of the Trinity in Catholic teaching is evi-
dent from the beginning of the Church. When Christ sent
the apostles forth to go and "make disciples of all nations"
(Mt 28:19), he instructed them to baptize in the name of the
Trinity: "baptizing them in the name of the Father, and of the
Son, and of the Holy Spirit" (Mt 28:19). From the earliest

centuries of the Church, and in the most ancient professions of faith, we find a belief in the Trinity of the Father, the Son, and the Holy Spirit. The Quicumque Creed (more popularly known as the Athanasian Creed), which dates from the fourth century, declares: "Now the Catholic faith is this: that we worship one God in the Trinity, and the Trinity in unity. ...The Father is a distinct person, the Son is a distinct person, and the Holy Spirit is a distinct person, but the Father and the Son and the Holy Spirit have one divinity, equal glory and co-eternal majesty."

The preface for the Mass on Holy Trinity Sunday summarizes our belief in what God has told us about himself: "For what you have revealed to us of your glory we believe equally of your Son and of the Holy Spirit, so that, in the confessing of the true and eternal Godhead, you might be adored in what is proper to each Person, their unity in substance, and their equality in majesty" (Roman Missal).

The revelation of the Trinity begins when Jesus told us that he is God's Son. Jesus teaches us that God is not only the Creator of the universe but also the Father of the eternally begotten Son, who became one with us as the God-man Jesus Christ. As Matthew's Gospel teaches us, "No one knows the Son except the Father, and no one knows the Father except the Son and anyone to whom the Son wishes to reveal him" (11:27).

Throughout history there have been countless claims of heaven touching earth, which reflects the longing of the human heart for God's presence. Yet we know that the emptiness spoken about by the prophets and reflected upon by wise men finds its fullness and satisfaction only in Jesus Christ, God and man, our Brother and Savior. Jesus is God's Son, and his revelation to us is that the great name of God is "Father."

JESUS WAS CRUCIFIED, DIED, WAS BURIED, AND ROSE

In one of the most familiar and cherished forms of the Way of the Cross, we find this invitation to prayer: "We adore you, O Christ, and we praise you." To which the people reply, "Because by your holy cross, you have redeemed the world." In this brief invitatory and response, Saint Alphonsus Liguori captures the essence of the article of the Creed that proclaims Jesus Christ "suffered under Pontius Pilate, was crucified, died and was buried."

There is much more to this statement of faith than the simple recognition that Christ died. If by his cross Christ had not redeemed us, his death would have had little meaning. With the eyes of faith, the apostles and all the believers after them gaze on the cross and see much more than just the instrument on which Jesus hung until he died.

The fact of Jesus's death is the core of the historical account and personal witness found in Matthew, Mark, Luke, and John. It is also referred to in other parts of the New Testament. Jesus was arrested, tried, sentenced, executed by crucifixion, and was buried.

The Gospel accounts are not news reports like the ones we see in newspapers or on television. The historical fact of Jesus's death must be understood through the eyes of faith. The Passion narratives report an actual event, but with the primary purpose of providing its theological significance and meaning. In other words, the death of Jesus is a theological reality that can be interpreted only with eyes of faith.

With simple but firm conviction, the Creed affirms, "On the third day he rose again." The Resurrection is the central mystery of our faith. It is an utterly astounding truth, because we have no point of reference against which to measure a rising to new life like Jesus's resurrection.

The story of Jesus should have concluded when he was placed in the tomb. Yet for the apostles and for us it was only the beginning. The life, teaching, ministry, and promises of Jesus are all verified and authenticated in his resurrection. His kingdom is real and is unfolding in our very world through the power of his rising from the dead.

In just one generation after the resurrection of Jesus, Saint Paul could write to the Corinthians that he was passing on to them "what I also received: that Christ died for our sins in accordance with the scriptures; that he was buried; that he was raised on the third day in accordance with the scriptures" (1 Cor 15:3-4). Paul is calling the attention of the Church to the living tradition passed on from those who saw the risen Lord. He is speaking of an established, verifiable tradition within the lifetime of people who could vouch for what they had seen and what they had preached. We are dealing with a real person, and there is continuity between the person who was taken down from the cross, wrapped in the shroud, and placed in the tomb and the one who is now risen from the dead and who appeared to numerous people.

Saint Paul continues by pointing to the number of witnesses. The risen Lord "appeared to Cephas, then to the Twelve. After that, he appeared to more than five hundred brothers at once, most of whom are still living, though some have fallen asleep. After that, he appeared to James, then to all the apostles. Last of all, as to one born abnormally, he appeared to me" (1 Cor 15:5-8). Paul is reminding us that there is an unbroken line, and not a very long one at that, from those who could bear witness to the Lord's resurrection because they had seen him alive in Paul's own day. He is speaking of living, verifiable people in the community who could say: "I know Jesus; I am his disciple; I was with him when he died. I have seen him after his resurrection. Jesus is alive!"

As the propositions for the synod were being prepared, there was strong and consistent support that the *kerygmatic* dimension of the New Evangelization be highlighted. It was precisely this citation from Corinthians that was added in its entirety to Proposition 9. In that proposition we read: "The 'first proclamation' is where the kerygma, the message of salvation of the paschal mystery of Jesus Christ, is proclaimed with great spiritual power to the point of bringing about repentance of sin, conversion of hearts, and a decision of faith. At the same time, there has to be a continuity between first proclamation and catechesis which instructs us in the deposit of the faith" (Prop. 9: New Evangelization and Initial Proclamation).

As Blessed John Paul II reaffirmed in his encyclical letter *Dives in Misericordia* (*"Rich in Mercy"*): "The fact that Christ 'was raised on the third day' (1 Cor 15:4) constitutes the final sign of the messianic mission, a sign that perfects the entire revelation of merciful love in a world that is subject to evil. At the same time it constitutes the sign that foretells 'a new heaven and a new earth' (Rv 21:1), when God 'will wipe away every tear from their eyes, there will be no more death, or mourning, no crying or pain, for the former things have passed away' (Rv 21:4)" (8).

Jesus not only rose from the dead, but he promised that we would also share in his resurrection. Easter is not so much a time of historical reflection as it is one of rejoicing in our own hope of resurrection. While it is true that we look to the past and see in Christ's risen life new and eternal existence, we do so to confirm our own faith that some day we too shall rise from the dead.

The Kerygma — the Core of the Good News

As Christ's message was more fully understood, it be-came evident that Jesus offers us not only a new way of living, but also a whole new way of being.

SUMMARY

The human heart longs for the presence of God, and the Christian life is defined by our experience of and relationship with Jesus Christ. The central doctrine of the Catholic faith is the mystery of the Holy Trinity which Jesus revealed to us through the sacred Scriptures. Proclaiming the Good News of the Paschal Mystery with zeal — Christ's crucifixion, death and resurrection — is at the very heart of the New Evangelization.

FOR REFLECTION

How have you come to know and love Jesus in your life? When have you most needed your faith? How has your relationship with God grown through the years?

CHAPTER 4

✠

The Church — Home of the Good News

The New Evangelization is about deepening our own faith, gaining confidence in the truth of that faith, and then sharing it with others. The Church is essential to all three of these elements.

The Church is the home of the Good News. What the Church proclaims about Jesus Christ is true. We can have confidence in our faith that comes to us in and through the Church. Our efforts at the New Evangelization must include a clear awareness of the Church and why Jesus established this sacred means to carry on his work.

The synod spoke of this article of faith in these words: "The particular church, led by the bishop, who is helped by priests and deacons, with the collaboration of consecrated persons and the laity, is the subject of the New Evangelization. This is so because in each place, the particular church is the concrete manifestation of the Church of Christ and as such initiates, coordinates, and accomplishes the pastoral actions through which the New Evangelization is carried out" (Prop 41: New Evangelization and the Particular Church).

Thus the deepening of our faith today brings with it a renewal in our understanding of the essential role of the Church. We profess our faith in God the Father, in his only begotten Son, and in the Holy Spirit. But the same Creed calls upon us to profess our faith in the one, holy, catholic, and apostolic Church. It is in and through the Church that we hear and appropriate the words of everlasting life.

The Church, as the Body of Christ and the people of God, is structured, visible, and identifiable. It carries on the unique work of Christ. As the *Catechism of the Catholic Church* quotes the Second Vatican Council: "'The one mediator, Christ, established and ever sustains here on earth his holy Church, the community of faith, hope, and charity as a visible organization through which he communicates truth and grace to all men' (*Lumen Gentium*, 8). The Church is at the same time: a 'society structured with hierarchical organs and the mystical body of Christ; the visible society and the spiritual community; the earthly Church and the Church endowed with heavenly riches' (*LG*, 8)" (771).

The Lord Jesus endowed his community with a structure that will remain until the Kingdom is fully achieved. He purposefully chose the Twelve, with Saint Peter as their head, as the foundation stones of "the new Jerusalem" (cf. Mt 19:28). The apostles and the other disciples share in Christ's mission and his power precisely to lead and serve his new Body, so that together through works of faith and love the kingdom of God may become manifest in our world.

Her members also name the Church "Holy Mother Church" because in the Sacrament of Baptism she gives us new life, and in the other sacraments she nurtures, sustains, heals, and sanctifies our spiritual life. The Church is called mother because, by virtue of Christ's love, she gives birth to many children. All the faithful are born of her: "By her preaching and by baptism she brings forth to a new and immortal life children who are conceived of the Holy Spirit and born of God" (*LG*, 64). As Saint Cyprian expressed it so clearly centuries ago, "You cannot have God for your father if you have not the Church for your mother" (*On the Unity of the Catholic Church*, 6).

In response to the question "How do we come to know and encounter Jesus today?" we look to the Church. The answer is found in the only living witness to the Lord Jesus, the only witness who can say I was there when Jesus died, when he rose, when he ascended into heaven, and when he sent the gift of the Holy Spirit on it. That one remaining living witness is Christ's body, his Church. It is in living continuity with that Church that you and I find our connectedness to the Gospels and to Christ himself.

APOSTOLIC TRADITION

How does the teaching of Christ get from him to us? How can we claim truly to know Jesus? These are important questions that we must answer when we recognize that God spoke in and through Jesus Christ twenty centuries ago yet intended the message for each of us today. The reality through which we ensure our continuity with the Lord is called Apostolic Tradition. It is best described as the passing on, under the inspiration of the Holy Spirit, what Jesus said and did. What makes it unique is that the very passing on in this way guarantees that the saving story of Jesus is not forgotten, misunderstood, or lost from age to age, from generation to generation, from person to person.

As the Second Vatican Council teaches, "the apostles took care to appoint successors in this hierarchically structured society" (*LG*, 20). This apostolic succession is noted by the earliest Fathers of the Church who lived at the end of the apostolic age. Pope Saint Clement of Rome, writing around the year A.D. 96, says that the apostles themselves "laid down a rule once for all to this effect: when these men died, other approved men should succeed to their sacred ministry" (*Letter to the Corinthians*).

It is only through this uninterrupted tradition, stretching back to the time of the apostles and continued by their successors, the bishops, that we can be sure of the integrity and validity of the Christian faith. The Church is called "apostolic" precisely because she alone can trace her origins to the deposit of faith entrusted to the apostles, the Twelve, chosen by Jesus and charged, together with their successors, with the responsibility of teaching the true faith, making sure that it is presented clearly, and applying it to the problems and needs of every age. In this way, we have a guarantee that what is taught today is what Jesus actually taught and intended as guidance for his followers. We believe that nothing is forgotten, misunderstood, or lost from century to century, from generation to generation, from person to person.

The prophetic mission of the College of Bishops cannot be grasped, though, exclusively as a pragmatic need for internal organization and theological coherence. Ultimately, it can be understood only in the context of revelation itself, when revealed truth is perceived as salvific and the reliable transmission of that truth as a precious gift from the Lord entrusted to the Church. Only the Holy Spirit, dwelling within the Church, can make possible the teaching ministry of the bishop.

The magisterium, the Church's teaching office, does not assert that in its proclamation of the faith it has exhausted every development, nuance, or application of the faith in the circumstances of our day. But the Church does define that the authoritative teachers of the faith will not lead us into error and away from Christ. No one else can rightfully make that claim. We turn to the teaching of the Church not for speculation, but for sure guidance on the way to eternal life with Christ.

God's Family

Jesus invites us into God's family. Jesus is the "only Son of God" (Jn 3:18). We receive our status by adoption. "As proof that you are children, God sent the spirit of his Son into our hearts, crying out, 'Abba Father!' So you are no longer a slave but a child, and if a child then also an heir, through God" (Gal 4:6-7).

"Why do you call us brothers and sisters?" a youngster asked me after Mass. "You're not my brother." "Ah, but I am spiritually, because we are all members of God's family," I responded. After he received a nod of affirmation from his mother and father who stood behind him, he said, "Wow, I didn't know that." Then he added, "That's cool," offering his youthful declaration of approval.

Each of us, in fact, is a member of God's family, God's people. Clearly we belong to our own natural family, and then because of baptism we belong to God's family. Together we are real spiritual brothers and sisters.

Like any family, the Church also faces challenges. In the last decades some have chosen to leave home. Some may say they are "spiritual" but not "religious," and therefore not affiliated with the Church. Others may never have really known what the family is all about. And still others may have had a bad experience.

The family of God is called his Church. Its members, those baptized into the Church, you and I, form a body with

Christ as its head. In order to truly know Christ, one must know him in his Body, the Church.

Saint Paul takes this for granted when he calls us, as he did the first disciples, "to live in a manner worthy of the call you have received ... striving to preserve the unity of the spirit through the bond of peace: one body and one Spirit ... one Lord, one faith, one baptism" (Eph 4:1-5).

The Second Vatican Council, which was convoked fifty years ago by Blessed John XXIII, chose in a particular way to speak of the Church as the "people of God" (see *LG*, 9-17). The Church is not an abstraction or a mere human institution. The new Body of Christ is made up of all the members of the family of faith who are blessed with the gifts of the Spirit and are united as one body around the apostles and their successors, with Christ as its head.

In the midst of the Synod on the New Evangelization, Pope Benedict celebrated Mass for a huge throng in Saint Peter's Square. At the Mass were present, reflecting on the Second Vatican Council's emphasis on the restoration of unity among all Christians, Ecumenical Patriarch Bartholomew I, head of the Orthodox Church, and Archbishop Rowan Williams, the archbishop of Canterbury and head of the Anglican Communion. This was a symbolic renewal of reflection on the importance of the Second Vatican Council and what has happened in the meantime. In the context of that Mass, the Holy Father spoke about the importance of the council as the source of ongoing renewal in the Church.

The pope said: "If we place ourselves in harmony with the authentic approach which Blessed John XXIII wished to give to Vatican II, we will be able to realize it during this Year of Faith, following the same path of the Church as she continuously endeavors to deepen the deposit of faith entrusted to her by Christ. ... If today the Church proposes a new Year of Faith and a new evangelization, it is not to honor [the] anniversary [of Vatican II], but because there is more need of it, even more than there was fifty years ago! And the reply to be given to this need is the one desired by the Popes, by the council fathers and contained in its documents."

The Church — Home of the Good News

The family of God is called his Church. Its members, those baptized into the Church, you and I, form a body with Christ as its head. In order to truly know Christ, one must know him in his Body, the Church.

SUMMARY

The Catholic Church carries on the unique work of Christ. We believe that, while he was on earth, Jesus established and structured his Church for the purpose of communicating truth and grace. The deposit of faith has been entrusted to the bishops, successors of the apostles, in the uninterrupted tradition of the Church. Together with all of the faithful, the Church is the fullest expression of the Body of Christ on earth. It is in and through the Church that we exercise our responsibilities for the New Evangelization.

FOR REFLECTION

Where did you learn the faith? Who are your faith models? What does it mean to say that the Catholic Church is the fullest expression of Christ's body on earth? How has your participation in the Church shaped your life?

CHAPTER 5

✠

The Church — Font of the New Evangelization

Each year, couples from all over the Washington archdiocese gather at a Mass in which we recognize their anniversaries, ranging from twenty-fifth to fiftieth and beyond. On rare occasions, we have celebrated seventieth wedding anniversaries.

In the reception line I often ask a senior couple, "What is the secret to your success?" The answers vary. But one that I will long remember came from a couple celebrating their fiftieth wedding anniversary. They told me that they have made it a practice every day of their married life to say a prayer together before they go to bed. "Otherwise," one of them noted, "we could forget that Jesus is a part of our love, our marriage, and our lives."

The Church and her sacraments are a continual reminder to us of God, God's love, and God's place in our lives. These great gifts to us from God are given precisely so that we never forget that God is a part of our love, our lives, all that we do.

The Synod on the New Evangelization makes clear that the Church is the place where the New Evangelization finds its home. Proposition 41, which begins the section entitled Agents/Participants of the New Evangelization, states: "The particular Church, led by the bishop, who is helped by priests and deacons, with the collaboration of consecrated persons and the laity, is the subject of the New Evangelization. This is

47

so because in each place, the particular Church (the diocesan Church) is the concrete manifestation of the Church of Christ and as such initiates, coordinates, and accomplishes the pastoral action through which the New Evangelization is carried out" (Prop. 41: New Evangelization and the Particular Church).

In the Acts of the Apostles, in which we recognize the beginning of the Church and the gathering together of people from every land and nation who will become one in the Holy Spirit, we read:

> We are Parthians, Medes, and Elamites,
> inhabitants of Mesopotamia, Judea and Cappadocia,
> Pontus and Asia, Phrygia and Pamphylia,
> Egypt and the districts of Libya near Cyrene,
> as well as travelers from Rome,
> both Jews and converts to Judaism, Cretans and Arabs,
> yet we hear them speaking in our own tongues
> of the mighty acts of God. (2:9-11)

In my words of welcome to Pope Benedict XVI at the beginning of Mass for nearly 50,000 people gathered at Nationals Park in Washington, D.C., in April 2008, I made reference to the same phenomenon taking place in our nation: "This Church from all of America — as it gathers in worship and seeks to reflect your call to be a people saved in hope — shows a face reflective of Africa, Central and South America, India, Asia, Europe as well as our own Native Americans and those who trace their families to people who came in successive waves of immigration going all the way back to the arrival of the first Catholics in this part of the world at Saint Mary's, Maryland."

In his homily, the pope went on to speak to us of our need to recognize the Church as the instrument of Christ's work in the world today, mediating the action of the Spirit for all of us. He invited us "to consider the growth of the Church in America as one chapter in the greater story of the Church's expansion following the descent of the Holy Spirit at Pentecost.... In every time and place, the Church is called to grow in unity through constant conversion to Christ, whose saving work is proclaimed by the successors of the apostles and celebrated in the sacraments. This unity, in turn, gives rise to an unceasing missionary outreach, as the Spirit spurs believers to proclaim 'the great works of God' and to invite all people to enter the community of those saved by the blood of Christ and granted new life in his Spirit."

How does all this happen? How is it that Christ continues to reach us in and through his Church and touch us in the sacraments? It is precisely in the outpouring of the Spirit upon the apostles and through them on the Church that this wondrous action of God continues to be present in our lives. The Holy Father continued in his homily with that reminder.

"Through the surpassing power of Christ's grace, entrusted to frail human ministers, the Church is constantly reborn and each of us is given the hope of a new beginning," he said. "Let us trust in the Spirit's power to inspire conversion, to heal every wound, to overcome every division, and to inspire new life and freedom."

When we read or hear proclaimed the signs and wonders of Jesus, we may be inclined to think that these Gospel accounts are events of the past. We are amazed, as the first disciples must have been, by the mystery of Jesus's life, passion, death, and resurrection.

However, Jesus desired not only to heal, to forgive, to draw people to himself in his day and time. His saving words and deeds were for all people of all time. And his saving work

— that is, the fullness of God's revelation — will endure till the end of time.

SACRAMENTS

The seven sacraments of the Catholic Church are the means by which Christ's redemptive work in his passion, death, and resurrection are present for all time and for all the faithful. The sacraments are the continuation, in every age, of the signs and wonders that Jesus worked while he walked on the earth some two thousand years ago. We believe that the sacraments are, as it were, arms of the Savior himself by which he extends his action throughout place and time to give life, to bless, to renew, to heal, and to multiply the bread of life.

The synod spoke insistently about the importance of the Church's sacraments and liturgy. In Proposition 35, we read that the liturgy "is, therefore, the primary and most powerful expression of the New Evangelization.... The liturgy is not just a human action but an encounter with God which leads to contemplation and deepening friendship with God. In this sense, the liturgy of the Church is the best school of the faith" (Prop. 35: Liturgy).

Baptism

Three of the sacraments — baptism, confirmation, and the Eucharist — are concerned with Christian initiation: "The three sacraments of Christian initiation closely combine to bring the faithful to the full stature of Christ and to enable them to carry out the mission of the entire people of God in the Church and in the world" (Congregation for Divine Worship and the Discipline of the Sacraments,

Rite of Baptism for Children, 1969, General Introduction, 2)

In its Proposition 38, the synod notes the key role of the sacraments of initiation in the New Evangelization. Here we read, "The synod wishes to state that Christian initiation is a crucial element in the New Evangelization and is the means by which the Church, as a mother, brings forth children and regenerates herself" (Prop. 38: Christian Initiation and the New Evangelization).

As Pope Benedict XVI teaches us in *Sacramentum Caritatis* (the apostolic exhortation "The Sacrament of Charity"):

> It must never be forgotten that our reception of baptism and confirmation is ordered to the Eucharist....The Sacrament of Baptism, by which we were conformed to Christ, incorporated in the Church and made children of God, is the portal to all the sacraments. (17)

Baptism makes us members of the Church. But to become a member of the Church is to be radically changed; it is to be grafted on the vine (cf. Jn 15:4-6) and joined vitally to the Body of Christ. Through an all-pervading bond of life, we become members of God's covenanted people. All this is effected in the Paschal Mystery: "This cup is the new covenant in my blood, which will be shed for you" (Lk 22:20).

Confirmation

Confirmation exists to extend to the Church of every time and place the gift of the Holy Spirit sent to the apostles on Pentecost. The Holy Spirit is the gift of Christ:

> And I will ask the Father, and he will give you an-

other Advocate to be with you always, the Spirit of truth.... The Advocate, the holy Spirit that the Father will send in my name — he will teach you everything and remind you of all that [I] told you.... When the Advocate comes whom I will send you from the Father ... he will testify to me. (Jn 14:16-17,26; 15:26)

Christ's promise was fulfilled for the apostles on Pentecost:

When the time for Pentecost was fulfilled, they were all in one place together. And suddenly there came from the sky a noise like a strong driving wind, and it filled the entire house in which they were. Then there appeared to them tongues as of fire, which parted and came to rest on each one of them. And they were all filled with the holy Spirit and began to speak in different tongues, as the Spirit enabled them to proclaim. (Acts 2:1-4)

Confirmation is thus the sacrament whereby the apostles and their successors, by the laying on of hands and anointing with chrism, communicate to the whole Church and all its members the gift of the Spirit received at Pentecost. It is Pentecost extended throughout the world, perpetuated, and made ever present in the Church. It is a call to spread the kingdom of Christ, to spread the message of salvation.

Confirmation implies growth, and it is a continual challenge to the recipient to cultivate growth. Life is required for this growth, and the recipient must be in the state of grace. Yet confirmation cannot be counted on to produce instantaneous growth; nor is it intended to do this. As one of the sacraments which are administered to a person only once, and whose effect is therefore permanent, confirmation confers a permanent character. This is shown by the words with which it is administered: "Be sealed with the gift of the Holy Spirit." We have heard Saint Paul speak of this seal; his words to the Corinthians, already quoted above, seem especially applicable to confirmation:

> But the one who gives us security with you in Christ and who anointed us is God; he has also put his seal upon us and given the Spirit in our hearts as a first installment. (2 Cor 1:21-22)

Eucharist

The Eucharist is at the heart of the Church's life. In the Eucharist, Christ himself is present to his people in the Paschal Mystery. Rich in symbolism and richer in reality, the Eucharist bears within itself the reality of Christ and mediates to us his saving work: "This most holy mystery," writes Pope Benedict XVI, "needs to be firmly believed, devoutly celebrated, and intensely lived in the Church" (*Sacramentum Caritatis*, 94).

The Second Vatican Council's *Sacrosanctum Concilium* (*Constitution on the Sacred Liturgy*) noted: "At the Last Supper, on the night he was betrayed, our Savior instituted the Eucharistic Sacrifice of his Body and Blood. He did this to perpetuate the sacrifice of the cross throughout the centuries until he should come again, and so to entrust to his beloved spouse, the Church, a memorial of his death and resurrection: a sacrament of love, a sign of unity, a bond of charity, a paschal banquet in which Christ is received, the mind is filled with grace, and a pledge of future glory is given to us" (47).

At the Last Supper, the Lord instituted a new memorial sacrifice. The true "Lamb of God" (John 1:29) was about to be slain. By his cross and resurrection, he was to free not just one nation from bondage but all humanity from the more bitter slavery of sin. He was about to create a new people of God by the rich gift of his Spirit. There was to be a new law of love, a new closeness to God, a new promised land. All was to be new when God fulfilled the promises of the centuries in the paschal mysteries.

Jesus became the new Passover, the unique and final sacrifice by which God's plan of salvation was accomplished. In God's holy plan, it was determined that the Word of God, made flesh in Jesus Christ, would be the expiatory sacrifice that would take away the sins of the world. In fact, we continue at the celebration of every Eucharist, in the holy sacrifice of the Mass, to proclaim before we receive the body and blood of Christ in Communion, "Behold the Lamb of God, behold him who takes away the sins of the world" (*Roman Missal*).

The sufferings of Jesus and the glory of his resurrection are inseparably joined in the Paschal Mystery. The preface for Easter proclaims, "By dying he destroyed our death and by rising he restored us to life." The Father saved us not only by delivering up his Son for us but also by raising him from the dead (cf. 1 Pt 1:3-5). It is for this reason that we say the cross of Christ points toward and is fulfilled in the Resurrection. The Paschal Mystery includes both the death and the Resurrection, both the expiation and the glorification, both the dying and the rising to new life.

The center of all Christian life is Christ himself. By his Incarnation and work of redemption, we are healed and called to share in a new life, a life that binds us together as children of God and sharers in the life of the Trinity.

The Second Vatican Council rightly proclaimed that the Eucharistic sacrifice is the "source and summit of the Christian life" (*LG*, 11). For in the Eucharist, Christ gives himself to us, and we lay hold of him. The Eucharist is not merely a symbol and ceremony; it is the Sacrament in which, most of all, the saving works of Jesus and the gifts of God are made accessible to men.

The faith of the Church in the real presence of Jesus in the Eucharist goes back to the words of Jesus himself as recorded in the Gospel of Saint John. In the Eucharistic discourse, after the multiplication of the loaves, Our Lord contrasted ordinary bread with the bread that is not of this world but that contains eternal life for those who eat it. He said, "I am the bread of life ... I am the living bread that came down from heaven; whoever eats this bread will live forever; and the bread that I will give is my flesh for the life of the world" (Jn 6:48-51).

The Eucharist brings about the nourishing effect it symbolizes. This is achieved through the presence of Jesus himself and the bestowal of grace on those who receive him according to their individual needs and the needs of the community. Insofar as we have been wounded by sin, Christ and his power work in a remedial way; to the extent that we are making progress in holiness, he strengthens and fosters our growth.

In his encyclical *Ecclesia de Eucharistia* (*On the Eucharist in Its Relationship to the Church*), Blessed John Paul II recalls that the Church's life and development are rooted in the sacrifice of the cross which is re-presented on the altar. The Holy Father reminds us that in the earliest chapters of the Acts of the Apostles, which describe the life of the ancient and fledgling Church, we find the description of the faithful coming together in order that they might devote themselves "to the teaching of the apostles and to the communal life, to the breaking of the bread and to the prayers" (2:42). The "breaking of the bread" refers to the Eucharist. Two thousand years later, we continue to relive that primordial image of the Church.

The Sacrament of the New Evangelization

Penance

There is still another sacrament that looms very large in the renewal of the life of the Church and particularly in the New Evangelization. Because of the importance of this sacrament and the emphasis given to it by the synod, I want to reflect at length on this extraordinary gift of God's mercy. Cardinal Timothy Dolan, archbishop of New York and president of the United States Conference of Catholic Bishops, suggested in the context of the synod that penance be seen as "the sacrament of the New Evangelization."

The synod recognizes the central place of the Sacrament of Reconciliation in the New Evangelization. As Proposition 33 states: "The Sacrament of Penance and Reconciliation is the privileged place to receive God's mercy and forgiveness. It is a place for both personal and communal healing. In this sacrament, all the baptized have a new and personal encounter with Jesus Christ, as well as a new encounter with the Church, facilitating a full reconciliation through the forgiveness of sins. Here the penitent encounters Jesus, and, at the same time, he or she experiences a deeper appreciation of himself or herself. The synod fathers ask that this sacrament be put again at the center of the pastoral activity of the Church" (Prop. 33: The Sacrament of Penance and the New Evangelization).

Why is it so difficult at times to be good and to do what is right? Even though we may have good intentions, why do we often find ourselves doing what we know we should not do, or failing to do the good we know we ought to do? These perplexing questions arise from our awareness that a part of us is determined to do good while at the same time an element within us continually turns away from the good we know we can do.

In the seventh chapter of his Letter to the Romans, Saint Paul describes this situation while writing about what we call the human condition: "What I do, I do not understand. For I do not do what I want, but I do what I hate. ... The willing is ready at hand, but doing the good is not. For I do not do the good I want, but I do the evil I do not want. Now if [I] do what I do not want, it is no longer I who do it, but sin which dwells within me" (7:15-20).

Saint Paul's cry from the heart is something each of us has experienced. Why is it that we have the best of intentions, sincerely make New Year's resolutions, firmly renew our aspirations, sometimes every day, and then allow the worst in us to come out?

We can find an explanation in the opening chapters of the Book of Genesis. A description of this seemingly relentless and endless struggle between good and evil is described in the imagery of the serpent tempting Adam and Eve with the forbidden fruit. God said, "You are free to eat from any of the trees of the garden except the tree of knowledge of good and evil. From that tree you shall not eat; when you eat from it you shall die" (2:16-17). The tempter, however, said: "You certainly will not die! God knows well that when you eat of it your eyes will be opened and you will be like gods, who know good and evil" (3:4-5).

Adam and Eve ate the forbidden fruit. They chose their own desires over God's will and plan. This teaching, whatever the imagery, is very clear. Sin entered the world through the decision of a human being to choose self over God and God's plan. God is not responsible for the evil in the world.

Each one of us is an heir to Adam and Eve. We are members of the human family. We trace our lineage back to this couple and their failure to respect God's law, will, and plan. The actions that they took shattered God's created harmony, not only for them but also for us. Their sin is reflected in us and is mirrored in our daily life. This helps to explain why it is so difficult to do good, to do what we know we should do.

Saint Paul describes the consequences of original sin within us as a struggle between the old person and the new person. The old person is interested only in the selfish man or woman who dwells within each of us. The life of the new person, baptized and alive in God's grace, is directed to God, Christ, and our neighbors. This struggle deep within our human nature has continued from the time of Adam and Eve's sin. Our baptism washes away original sin, but its effects still remain.

Yet we are not lost. We are not left to our own devices. Saint Paul, writing to the Corinthians, reminds us that in Adam, sin was introduced into the world and, through sin, death and all of its consequences. So, too, however, grace and new creation come to us in Christ. Just as death came through a human being, so, too, the resurrection of the dead came through a human being. As in Adam all people die, so in Christ all shall be brought to life — a fullness of life, a new creation already beginning in us through grace (cf. 1 Cor 15).

This is the message we proclaim when we face the mystery of sin, the reality of original sin, and the problems of the human condition that lead us to personal sin. Just as Adam brought sin, death, disharmony, confusion, disruption, and struggle into our lives, so, too, now Christ, the new Adam, gives us grace, redemption, new life, and salvation. It is in Jesus Christ that we now find the beginnings of the new creation. He leads us back to the Father, overcomes the tragic alienation of sin, and restores harmony. Jesus gives us newness of life in grace that begins to restore our relationship with God which will lead to full communion with God in glory. It is for this reason that we identify Christ as the new Adam. Grace is the beginning of a new creation for all of those baptized into Christ.

The Church believes in the forgiveness of sins. Jesus died to wash away all sin and he forgave sins not only in his public life but also after his resurrection. Jesus also extended to his Church the power to apply the redemption he won on the cross and the authority to forgive sin.

"The Light Is On for You"

A particularly effective pastoral initiative involving the Sacrament of Reconciliation is titled "The Light Is On for You." At the heart of this program recently endorsed by the United States Conference of Catholic Bishops is the commitment of a diocesan Church to see that on a specific evening during the week at a given time, confessions will be heard in all of the churches across the diocese. In this way, the people will have an opportunity, no matter where they are, to avail themselves of this sacrament.

The "Light Is On for You" pastoral initiative in the Archdiocese of Washington is accompanied by considerable advertisements, including on billboards and on buses and subway trains, and is usually held during the weeks of Lent. In a public way, the campaign highlights the importance of the Sacrament of Penance and our need for God's help, love, and mercy. Some people have experienced the joy of returning to the sacrament after not having gone to confession for decades. The symbol of the light on in churches provides people with a beacon of hope, reconciliation, and absolution. One priest commented: "By simply extending that unique invitation, their hearts had been touched. In the voice of the Church, they heard the voice of the Father himself saying, 'Come back home.' And they came!" For more information about this pastoral initiative, see www.thelightison.org.

The *Catechism of the Catholic Church* points out that our faith in the forgiveness of sins is tied in with faith in the Holy Spirit, the Church and the Communion of Saints. "It was when he gave the Holy Spirit to his apostles that the risen Christ conferred on them his own divine power to forgive sins: 'Receive the Holy Spirit. If you forgive the sins of any, they are forgiven; if you retain the sins of any, they are retained' (Jn 20:22-23)" (976).

Fully conscious that only God forgives sins, we bring our failings to the Church because Jesus imparted to his apostles his own power to forgive sins. In doing this, Jesus gave to his Church the authority to restore and reconcile the sinner with God and also with the ecclesial community, the Church. This ecclesial dimension is expressed most forcefully in Christ's words to Simon Peter: "I will give you the keys to the kingdom of heaven. Whatever you bind on earth shall be bound in heaven; and whatever you loose on earth shall be loosed in heaven" (Mt 16:19).

In the simple actions of contrition, confession, absolution, and satisfaction we are restored to a whole new life. It remains one of the great marvels of God's love that God would make forgiveness so readily available to each of us.

THE STORY OF GOD'S LOVE

The Sacrament of Reconciliation is the story of God's love that never turns away from us. It endures even our shortsightedness and selfishness. Like the father in the parable of the prodigal son, God waits, watches and hopes for our return every time we walk away. Like the son in the parable, all we need to do to return to our Father is to recognize our wrong and seek God's love. Jesus continues to speak to us of our noble calling to holiness and of his loving forgiveness. He offers us reconciliation if we ask for it.

Apart from the Eucharist, there simply is no greater gift that the Church can give her people than the gift of reconciliation. As the synod fathers noted, penance is the sacrament of the New Evangelization because it offers us "a new and personal encounter with Jesus Christ, as well as a new encounter with the Church." The light of God's love, of God's mercy, of God's forgiveness, is always on, and we can always come home to God, and to the Church. We may have been away for a long time, or we may have been there all along but recognize our need to find new life in Christ through this sacrament of healing and hope.

The deepest spiritual joy each of us can sense is the freedom from whatever would separate us from God and the restoration of our friendship with such a loving and merciful Father who receives each of us with all the forgiveness and love he lavished on the prodigal son. Renewed, refreshed, and reconciled in this sacrament, we who have sinned become a "new creation." And with this new life in Christ, we, as his disciples, can go forth and share our faith with others.

The Church — Font of the New Evangelization

We believe that the sacraments are, as it were, arms of the Savior himself, by which he extends his action throughout place and time to give life, to bless, to renew, to heal, and to multiply the bread of life.

SUMMARY

Each of the sacraments has a distinct and essential role in the New Evangelization. Baptism, confirmation and the Eucharist — the sacraments of Christian initiation — are highlighted as the foundation for the work of evangelization because they contain and realize the full reality of Jesus Christ. The Sacrament of Penance is central to the New Evangelization in that it offers us "a new and personal encounter with Jesus Christ, as well as a new encounter with the Church, facilitating a full reconciliation through the forgiveness of sins." Our experience of God's grace in the sacraments prepares us to go forth and share our faith with others.

FOR REFLECTION

How do the sacraments nourish and sustain your faith? Why has the Sacrament of Penance been called "the sacrament of the New Evangelization"? What is the connection between evangelizing or sharing our faith and confessing our sins?

CHAPTER 6

✠

Parishes — Centers of the
New Evangelization

The New Evangelization can be the outlook that impels all of us to discover fresh resources, to open original avenues, and to summon new strength to advance the Good News of the Lord. We cannot simply invite from a distance. Instead, we search actively and carefully for our sisters and brothers who are away from the practice of their faith.

This brings us to a reflection on where the Church, alive in faith and love, does the work of the New Evangelization. The synod spoke of a wide range of "places" of the New Evangelization and how this graced work is the fruit of the Holy Spirit. In Proposition 43, we read what is really a reflection on the many gifts of the Spirit that are poured out on the Church: "The Holy Spirit directs the Church in her mission of evangelization 'with various hierarchical and charismatic gifts' (*LG*, 4). In fact the dioceses are 'a portion of the people of God under the pastoral care of the bishop, helped by his presbyterate' (*Christus Dominus*, 11), where the diverse charismatic realities recognize the authority of the bishop as integral to their own proper action in service of the ecclesial mission" (Prop. 43: Hierarchical and Charismatic Gifts).

At the same time, the synod goes on to remind us that since the Second Vatican Council, the New Evangelization has greatly benefited from the dynamism of the new ecclesial movements and new communities. Here the synod has reflected on how effective the ecclesial movements and the new communities are in bringing people back to the practice of the faith.

Parishes, gathered in communion with the bishop, are called to be centers of the New Evangelization. The synod reflected on the importance of the different places in the dioceses where the New Evangelization takes place. Of central importance is the parish. In Proposition 26, we read, "The bishops gathered in synod affirm that the parish continues to be the primary presence of the Church in neighborhoods, the place and instrument of Christian life, which is able to offer opportunities for dialogue among men, for listening to and announcing the Word of God, for organic catechesis, for training in charity, for prayer, adoration, and joyous Eucharistic celebrations" (Prop. 26: Parishes and Other Ecclesial Realities).

INDICATORS OF VITALITY

One of the signs of the spiritual strength of the Church is the vitality of its parishes. In Proposition 44, we read, "The parish, in and through all of its activities, should animate its members to become agents of the New Evangelization, witnessing through both their words and their lives" (Prop. 44: New Evangelization in the Parish).

In some parishes, a self-assessment takes place that allows the pastor and parish leadership, together with the faithful, to plan for the future while also identifying and addressing more immediate needs. This program, known as the Indicators of Vitality, allows parish-rooted discernment based on identifiable, objective norms in the areas of worship, education, community life, service, and administration.

The Indicators of Vitality is a tool developed by

the Archdiocese of Washington in service of the New Evangelization. More information about this pastoral initiative can be found at http://indicatorsofvitality.org. The text of the pastoral letter "Disciples of the Lord: Sharing the Vision" discussing the New Evangelization and describing the Indicators of Vitality can be found at http://adw.org/disciplesofthelord.pdf.

This program can assist in examining and assessing the ways in which the Church, manifested in its many parishes, worships, calls people to conversion, and exercises stewardship of God's gifts. In so doing, parishes are better equipped to carry out the work of the New Evangelization. In the words of the prophet Ezekiel, "The lost I will seek out, the strayed I will bring back, the injured I will bind up, the sick I will heal … shepherding them rightly" (Ez 34:16).

Yes, the light of Christ already shines brightly in each parish. Yet all of us recognize there is more to be done. Our efforts at a New Evangelization call us to look deeper into the vitality of our faith as it is expressed and lived in our parishes and in the homes of the faithful.

We should not be surprised that the first indicator of vitality — *worship* — relates to liturgy, sacraments, renewal efforts, devotions, prayer, and other such opportunities provided by the parish. We can readily see how significant liturgy is. We come together so that we might not only profess our faith and listen to the Scriptures, but also to worship the Father as Christ's new Body — members and Head.

Religion at its core is the quest for God. "One thing I ask of the Lord; / this I seek: / To dwell in the Lord's house / all the days of my life" (Ps 27:4). In a special way, this personal quest for God is concentrated in prayer; our personal prayer widens out to join with that of our fellow brothers and sisters in community prayer. When community prayer is the prayer of the living Church itself, gathering people into one in new ways, it becomes liturgy. Liturgy is the "public worship performed by the Mystical Body of Jesus Christ, that is, by the head and his members" (*Sacrosanctum Concilium*, 7).

A second indicator of vitality is *education*. Here we look at all of the efforts to ensure that ongoing faith formation in the belief and teachings of the Catholic Church are provided to parishioners of all ages. Catholic education in all of its forms has as its primary task communication of the person and message of Christ to adults, youth, and children. This unfolds through a wide range of efforts, but the goal is always the same. In our Catholic elementary and secondary schools, parish religious education programs, adult faith formation, the Rite of Christian Initiation for Adults, sacramental formation programs, and the many forms of youth ministry and evangelizing outreach, the threads of the encounter with Christ and his life-giving message are woven into the fabric of our human experience.

Community life is another gauge of parish vitality. It relates to a parish's efforts to build a sense of community by actively including all members of the parish, by reaching out to Catholics who may have fallen away from active membership in the Church and to those in the local community who do not belong to any church, and by recognizing the diversity of talents and needs of the parishioners.

In his encyclical *Deus Caritas Est* (*"God is Love"*), Pope Benedict XVI spoke of three essential elements of the life of the Church: "The Church's deepest nature is expressed in her threefold responsibility: of proclaiming the word of God (*kerygma-martyria*), celebrating the sacraments (*leitourgia*), and exercising the ministry of charity (*diakonia*)" (25). Thus we see *service* as another indicator of vitality. This dimension of parish life includes serving the poor, the marginalized, elderly, hurting families, and other needy people in the community both in and beyond the parish. It is in this area of parish life that peace, justice, and advocacy for those in need are actively pursued.

Finally, we come to *administration* and those aspects of Church life such as leadership, stewardship, management and decision-making processes of the parish, as well as the relationship of the parish to the rest of the Church.

As our efforts at the New Evangelization develop, my hope is that every parish, faith community, and program, both archdiocesan and local, will utilize the Indicators of Vitality as a measuring stick not only for our collective effectiveness but also for our own personal growth.

CATHOLIC EDUCATION

The synod also paid great attention to schools and education. In Proposition 27, we read, "Education is a constitutive dimension of evangelization." This proposition then highlights the critical value of schools in the process. "Children, teenagers, and young people have a right to be evangelized and educated. The schools and Catholic universities respond in this way to this need" (Prop. 27: Education). The synod thus calls us to see how important schools and Catholic education are to the New Evangelization.

In our structured, organized religious education efforts, Christ's voice is heard today and his Gospel announced. Perhaps it is for this reason that during his visit to the United States Pope Benedict addressed Catholic educators at The Catholic University of America and spoke so encouragingly about the ministry of education. He said: "Education is integral to the mission of the church to proclaim the Good News. First and foremost every Catholic educational institution is a place to encounter the living God, who in Jesus Christ reveals his transforming love and truth" (cf. *Spe salvi*, 4).

Our children today, as they grow up in an ever more complex world, need to be firmly grounded in knowledge of the authentic faith the Church professes. Then they can be prepared to live a full, happy, and holy life in communion with Christ.

Catholic schools are identified as Catholic through the presence of an approved religious education/faith formation program that ensures that the faith is integrated into and permeates the whole educational process at the school. Catholic identity also is visible in pastoral ministry programs that nurture personal spirituality and formation of the students into a living experience and witness of Christian life.

At every level — in Catholic elementary and secondary schools, and in Catholic institutions of higher education — the schools, with our support, must continue to do all that it takes to meet the challenge of presenting an educational alternative that is rooted in, and takes its daily inspiration from, the faith and in visible connectedness with the Church. Our education effort derives from our conviction that our Catholic faith invites us into dialogue with God and offers us a way of life grounded in his word. Even in a culture that denies the need for this dialogue, there is a deep yearning in the human heart for just such a conversation with God. Our role in Catholic education is to provide a frame of reference for a life that reflects the words of everlasting life.

The proposition on education ended with a statement about what we must do to support the critical role of Catholic schools in fostering the New Evangelization.

"The synod:
- Encourages Catholic educational institutions to do all that is possible to preserve their identity as ecclesial institutions;
- Invites all teachers to embrace the leadership which is theirs as baptized disciples of Jesus, giving witness through their vocation as educators;
- Urges particular Churches, religious families, and all those who have responsibility in the educational institutions, to facilitate the co-responsibility of laypeople, offering adequate formation and accompaniment for this" (Prop. 27: Education).

CATECHESIS AND CATECHISTS

In its discussion on education, the synod also identified the importance of catechesis, catechists, and the *Catechism* as sources for the New Evangelization. In Proposition 29, the synod writes: "Good catechesis is essential for the New Evangelization. The synod calls attention to the indispensable service that catechists provide the ecclesial communities and expresses profound gratitude for their dedication" (Prop 29: Catechesis, Catechists and the Catechism).

Catechists and those responsible for parish religious education share in one of the essential ministries of the Church — teaching the faith. Catechetical ministry in all its forms can claim to participate in the perennial task that traces its origins to the tradition of the apostles just as it can claim that its message is that which comes to us from the apostles. In this sense, the catechist is part of a great chain of living continuity that reaches back to the apostolic Church and reaches out to those today who need to hear and be formed in that life-giving word. It is easy to see why the Church places so much emphasis on the catechist.

The catechist, through his or her words and deeds, bears witness to Jesus, tells the story of Jesus, lives the message of Jesus. Teacher is an ancient and well-honored title. The teacher is the storyteller of the faith family. He or she passes on the collective memory of the community, the deposit of faith, so that each generation can benefit from the living faith of the past generations. This is especially important for those catechists and leaders of religious education who minister to our children, both in grade school and high school levels. The catechist can be "leaven" by bringing to those being formed in the faith an awareness of their own potential to change the world in which we live, and make it more truly a reflection — a manifestation — of God's kingdom among us.

In parishes we see more and more that the faithful have a vital role in the work of catechesis. It is not confined or reserved solely to clergy, catechists, and teachers. Increasingly, there is an affirmation of the principles articulated in the *General Directory for Catechesis* that "catechesis is a responsibility of the entire Christian community." The same directory instructs us that "Christian initiation indeed 'should not be the work of catechists and priests alone, but of the whole community of the faithful' " (220).

The entire faith community must be invited to evangelize and catechize, and also to be committed deeply in this effort. This is perhaps the most challenging aspect of the catechetical renewal today. All of us together must assume responsibility for sharing with others the faith that we have received and so cherish. Indeed, we see not only in the United States, but also around the world, the work that so many lay catechists do in passing on the faith.

However, ecclesial catechesis is not an undifferentiated or non-directed activity. The bishop, as head of a local Church, has the primary responsibility for catechesis in the particular church. This he does by being actively engaged in the teaching of the faith where this is possible, and certainly through the oversight of all who teach the faith. By extension, this task falls also to each priest by virtue of his ordination.

A number of priests have told me that they regularly use the bulletin as a catechetical tool. Their own more active engagement in the oversight of the various catechetical initiatives of the parish is another testimony to priestly teaching. Still others highlight their teaching presence in the parish utilizing the pulpit and Sunday liturgy homily.

THE CATECHISM OF THE CATHOLIC CHURCH

The synod also highlighted the value of the *Catechism of the Catholic Church* and its compendium, especially in the area of adult catechesis. The U.S. bishops determined that there was a noticeable absence of appropriate catechetical materials for many young adults, participants in the Rite of Christian Initiation of Adults, and those in parish and diocesan adult faith formation programs. Thus the bishops set out to produce a catechism that would be inviting, engaging and instructive — the *United States Catholic Catechism for Adults*. The goal was to have a catechism for adults that would be complete, but not necessarily encyclopedic, authentic in its content, and presented in a format that would appeal to young adult readers and learners today.

For its source material, the adult catechism turns to the

larger and more encyclopedic *Catechism of the Catholic Church*. The foundation on which the catechism rests is the teaching of Jesus as contained in the pages of sacred Scripture and the living tradition of the Church, and articulated in the magisterium, the teaching office of the bishops. It is also found in the writings of the Fathers of the Church and the saints who have lived out the faith in loving response to the will of God.

In describing the value of the *Catechism of the Catholic Church*, Pope John Paul II pointed out that it "is offered to every individual who asks us to give an account of the hope that is in us (cf. 1 Pt 3:15) and who wants to know what the Catholic Church believes" (*Fidei Depositum*, apostolic constitution on the publication of the *Catechism of the Catholic Church*, 4). The same can be said for the catechism for adults discussed here. It is meant to help us understand our faith better so that we, in turn, can help others accept the truth of our faith. The classical word for this effort is apologetics. It refers to the discipline that is concerned with the defense of or proof for Christianity.

Among the best qualities of the *U.S. Catholic Catechism for Adults* is its readability. Each chapter begins with a story based on a figure from sacred Scripture or, for the most part, from the history of the Church in the United States. We are then led into a reflection on some relevant element of the Creed, the celebration of the liturgy, the life of a Christian, or prayer.

The catechism for adults does more, however, than just present the faith. It strives to invite the reader into the particular element of faith treated in each specific chapter and to assist in the reader's faith journey with appropriate reflections, prayer, and an application of the faith to some special aspect of our culture that today challenges what we believe. The layout of the book is not only inviting, but it is a useful tool for helping the learner experience a living faith — the Church's faith.

Essentially, a catechism is a means to an end. God gives us the gift of faith, and the Church nurtures and sustains that faith through her teaching and sacramental ministry. A catechism is a tool or instrument for those involved in teaching the faith, and we all know how important it is to have the right tool. Whether we intend to work in the yard, kitchen, or workshop, if we have the right tool, the task is a lot easier.

In an age that has come to think of the teaching of the Church as a cafeteria line where one picks and chooses what one wants to believe, the catechism is a reminder that the whole meal is necessary for a well-balanced spiritual diet. The catechism provides completeness.

It is also authentic. Its content is not someone's opinion about what the Church believes or should believe. It is the true teaching of the Catholic Church proclaimed with authority by those who are responsible for guarding the integrity of the faith. The *U.S. Catholic Catechism for Adults* represents the effort to present a complete and authoritative proclamation of the faith of the Catholic Church today in our culture.

Additional catechetical resources with which I have had the privilege of being associated are available through Our Sunday Visitor. These include the long-standing and well received *The Teaching of Christ: A Catholic Catechism for Adults*, now in its fifth edition and cross-referenced with the *Catechism of the Catholic Church*. Other works include *The Gift of Faith*, and more recently in both English and Spanish *The Sacraments: A Continuing Encounter with Christ* (2010).

Why do we need to know more about our faith? Why would someone want to spend time learning more about what we believe? Why would you want to take time studying more about your Catholic faith? There are two good and basic reasons to do this. One is so that we can live it more fully; and, two, so that we can share it more effectively with others.

Catholic education in all of its forms has as its primary task the communication of the person and message of Christ to adults, youth, and children. This unfolds through the wide range of efforts, but the goal is always the same. In our Catholic elementary and secondary schools, parish religious education programs, adult faith formation, the Rite of Christian Initiation of Adults, sacramental formation programs, and the many forms of youth ministry, campus ministry, and evangelizing outreach. In all of these, the threads of the encounter with Christ and his life-giving message are woven into the fabric of our human experience.

Parishes — Centers of the New Evangelization

To be sure, the light of Christ already shines brightly in each parish. Yet all of us recognize that there is more to be done. Our efforts at a New Evangelization call us to look deeper into the vitality of our faith as it is expressed and lived in our parishes and in the homes of the faithful.

SUMMARY

The spiritual strength of the parish is reflected in its liturgy and worship, religious education and formation, service, administration and stewardship, and through the overall community life of the faithful. Catholic schools are to be imbued with a clear Catholic identity that ensures the Faith permeates the whole educational process. Solid catechesis is necessary to the work of the New Evangelization with the entire faith community encouraged to pass on the Faith to future generations. A renewed emphasis on the Catechism of the Catholic Church *and the* United States Catholic Catechism for Adults *will help us live and share our faith more effectively each day.*

FOR REFLECTION

Why is it important to teach the Faith to the next generation? How are you called to serve your parish community? What are some new ways we might witness to our faith in the digital age?

CHAPTER 7

✠

The Theological Tasks of the New Evangelization

Another focus of the New Evangelization identified by the synod is the area of theological enterprise. In Proposition 30, we read: "Theology as the science of faith has an importance for the New Evangelization.... The Church appreciates and promotes research and the teaching of theology. Scientific theology has its own proper place in the university where it must carry out dialogue between faith and the other disciplines and the secular world. Theologians are called to carry out this service as part of the salvific mission of the Church. It is necessary that they think and feel with the Church (*sentire cum Ecclesia*)" (Prop. 30: Theology).

The theological task of the New Evangelization is a very important one. Concepts such as incarnation, resurrection, redemption, sacrament, and grace — core themes of theology used to explain our belief in Jesus Christ — have little meaning for the practicing Catholic and the fallen-away Catholic in a culture where rationalism prevails.

The temptation for the evangelizer, and perhaps for pastors, is to not confront these conceptual obstacles, but instead place focus and energies on more sociological priorities or pastoral initiatives, or even develop a vocabulary apart from our own theology.

While it is important that the New Evangelization be alert to the signs of the time and speak with a voice that

reaches people today, it must do so without losing its rooted-
ness in the great living faith tradition of the Church already
expressed in theological concepts.

THEOLOGICAL FOUNDATIONS

In our reflections on the New Evangelization, a number of
theological foundation stones stand out. I would like to touch
on four of them.

a) Anthropological Foundation of the New Evangelization
The word anthropology comes from the Greek word *anthropos*,
which means "man" in the generic sense. So, we use anthropology to describe our study of the human person. For a Christian
the true appreciation of who we are as human beings includes
the recognition of original sin, personal sin, redemption by Jesus
through his death and resurrection, and our new life through
the outpouring of the Holy Spirit. If we want to know who
we are as human beings, we need to start with the revelation
of our fall, our restoration in grace, and our new life in Christ.

If secularization, with its atheistic tendencies, removes
God from the equation, the very understanding of what it
means to be human is altered. Thus the New Evangelization
must point to the very origin of our human dignity, self-
knowledge, and self-realization. The fact that each person is
created in the image and likeness of God forms the basis for
declaring, for example, the universality of human rights. Here,
once again, we see the opportunity to speak with conviction
to a doubting community about the truth and integrity of
reality such as marriage, family, the natural moral order, and
an objective right and wrong.

The New Evangelization has to rest on the understanding that it is the Christian faith that offers us some understanding when we address the problem of evil, the reality of sin, the fall, and the call to new life. Evil and sin are indeed obstacles to the Gospel, but it is precisely the Gospel message that makes sense of the human condition and the possibility of a life that overcomes the inherent limitations of human frailty. Ultimately, the New Evangelization must rest on the recognition that it is in the light of Jesus Christ that we understand fully what it means to be human.

b) Christological Foundation of the New Evangelization
Christology is the study of the person of Jesus Christ. It is a theological explanation of who Christ is, his relationship to the Father, his divinity and humanity, and the reality of his death and resurrection. Christology is important for our faith because, as the Second Vatican Council, in its *Pastoral Constitution on the Church in the Modern World (Gaudium et Spes)*, stated quite clearly, "The truth is that only in the mystery of the incarnate Word does the mystery of man take on light" (22). At the center of Christian faith is Christ.

The New Evangelization is the reintroduction, the re-proposing, of Christ. But the Christ we proclaim is the Christ of revelation, the Christ understood in his Church, the Christ of tradition and not of personal, sociological, or aberrant theological creation. On our own, none of us could come to know the mind, heart, love, and identity of God. Jesus came to reveal the truth — about God and about ourselves.

c) The Ecclesiological Foundation of the New Evangelization
When we speak of ecclesiology, we refer to the study of the Church. As has been noted, the Church is the home of

the Good News; it is the family of God and the font of the
New Evangelization. But part of our understanding of what
the Church is includes the recognition that Christ continues his redeeming work through his Body, the Church. This
is critical to understanding what the Church is, and thus
how necessary the Church is for the New Evangelization.

The New Evangelization must provide a clear theological
explanation for the necessity of the Church for salvation. This
is a sensitive aspect of our preaching and too often has been ne-
glected in catechesis. Rampant in much of the revival culture of
today is the sentiment that salvation is achieved solely through
a personal relationship with Jesus apart from the Church. But
what needs to be emphasized and demonstrated is that Christ
meets us, wherever we are, in and through the Church.

The efforts of the New Evangelization must speak about
God's universal salvific will, and at the same time recognize
that Jesus has provided a clear and unique path to redemption
and salvation. The Church is not one among many ways to
reach God, all of them equally valid. While God does wish all
to be saved, it is precisely out of his universal salvific will that
God sent Christ to bring us to adoption and eventual eternal
glory.

d) Soteriological Foundations of the New Evangelization
The word soteriology means the study of the *soter*, the Greek
word for "savior." Soteriology is simply the study of what redemption in Jesus Christ means. At the end of time, when
Christ has come to pass judgment on all, and when those
who have died will rise again, the redemption of mankind
will be brought to its total fullness. But this world, and the
time of trial, ends for each person with death. The Church
speaks of the last things — death, judgment, heaven, hell.

Soteriology also recalls for us the Good News that the beginning of Jesus's kingdom is already here, present among us. We need to see our lives as part of the work of the kingdom of God coming to be now in its very beginnings. Yet we recognize that the fullness of the Kingdom is only when Jesus returns to claim it and all his followers.

Thus intrinsic to the understanding of God's presence with us today is the awareness of what we mean by his kingdom. In the New Testament, we find the Kingdom everywhere. From the beginning of when Jesus "began to preach," he announced that "the kingdom of heaven is at hand" (Mt 4:17). Jesus spoke of the Kingdom's subjects, its power, its boundaries, its duration.

As the *Catechism of the Catholic Church* teaches, Christ has established his kingdom on earth, though not yet in the fullness of its glory. It is here, but it is still growing. "At the end of time, the Kingdom of God will come in its fullness" (1060). In the meantime, "Christ the Lord already reigns through the Church" (680).

The four theological foundation blocks for the New Evangelization point out for us that whatever pastoral goals we set for re-proposing Christ to this age, we must do so firmly rooted in the Creed. This includes the biblical vision of man created in the image and likeness of God, as part of a creation that reflects God's wisdom and that recognizes a natural, moral order for man's activities. Marring this created beauty is sin and the egoism that has marked every successive generation. However, into this world God sent his Son to offer us new life. He established a Church to continue his living and saving presence. Our salvation is intimately related to our participation in the great sacrament that is the Church, through which we hope to manifest the kingdom coming to be now and realize our part in it in glory.

> ### The Theological Tasks of the New Evangelization
>
> While it is important that the New Evangelization be alert to the signs of the time and speak with a voice that reaches people today, it must do so without losing its rootedness in the great living faith tradition of the Church already expressed in theological concepts.

SUMMARY

Four of the theological foundations for the New Evangelization are:

- *Human persons were created in the image and likeness of God.*
- *Jesus Christ is the Son of God, who came to dwell among us, at once fully human and divine, who was crucified, died, and rose for the salvation of the world.*
- *We come to know and love Christ in and through the Catholic Church.*
- *We build the kingdom on earth so as to experience the fullness of the kingdom of God in the life to come.*

FOR REFLECTION

How do the core Catholic teachings — which we profess in the Creed at Mass on Sunday — form your values and beliefs? Why does it matter that we believe human beings were created in God's image? What does this basic belief tell us about how we should treat each other?

CHAPTER 8

✠

Sharing the Faith

On one occasion, when I visited the participants in the Rite of Christian Initiation for Adults program at our Cathedral Church, Saint Matthew the Apostle, I was surprised to see one young lady. On many occasions, I had seen her at Mass at the cathedral and had greeted her at the back of church at the end of Mass. I had assumed she was Catholic. As I expressed my joy at seeing her in the RCIA program, I also commented that I thought she was Catholic. I asked her, since I had seen her so many times over so many years at Mass, what took her so long to decide to enter the Church? She replied very simply, "No one ever asked me."

The third element in the New Evangelization is the willingness and desire to share the faith. This can take the form of an invitation to those who have never been received into the Church, as well as to those who were baptized Catholic but have simply drifted away from the practice of the faith.

There are numerous people, particularly in what we call the Western world, who have already heard of Jesus. Our challenge is to stir up again and rekindle in the midst of their daily life and concrete situation a new awareness and familiarity with Jesus. We are called not just to announce but to adapt our approach so as to attract and to urge an entire generation to find again the uncomplicated, genuine, and tangible treasure of friendship with Jesus.

But this sharing of the faith depends on us. All of us, in our own particular way, are agents of the New Evangelization. The synod made this clear.

As Proposition 57, the conclusion of the long reflection of the work of the synod, tells us: "'You will be my witnesses' (Acts 1:8). From the very beginning, the Church has understood her responsibility to pass on the Good News. The task of the New Evangelization, following in this apostolic tradition, is the transmission of the faith.... This faith cannot be transmitted in a life which is not modeled after the Gospel or a life which does not find its meaning, truth, and future based on the Gospel" (Prop. 57: The Transmission of the Christian Faith).

In this concluding section on the list of propositions, we read what is the closest thing to a definition of the elements that comprise the New Evangelization. Here we find that all action of the New Evangelization "calls all believers to renew their faith and in their personal encounter with Jesus Christ in the Church, to deepen their appreciation of the truth of the faith and joyfully to share it" (Prop. 57: The Transmission of the Christian Faith).

The first moment of any evangelization originates not from a program, but in an encounter with a person, Jesus Christ, the Son of God. The Church maintains that "it is the same Lord Jesus who, present in his Church, goes before the work of evangelizers, accompanies it, follows it, and makes their labors bear fruit. What took place at the origins of Christian history continues through its entire course" (Congregation for the Doctrine of the Faith, *Some Aspects of Evangelization*, 1).

We rely first and always on Jesus. He alone is the cornerstone. As we approach those who have grown cold or distant in their faith, the touchstone is the simplicity of instruction that motivates and speaks to the depth of the human person. We turn to our brothers and sisters who have received baptism and yet no longer participate in the life of the Church. To them we offer our experience of Jesus's love, not a philosophical thesis on behavior.

The personal witness of the follower of Jesus is itself a proclamation of the Word. Our message today must, therefore, be grounded in the testimony of our lives. These are also moments to invite, not to scold.

To our world we need to communicate our own joy of being definitively and completely loved by Christ. In this we are, therefore, capable of loving others. Our communication should be in words and in life, in prayer and in deed, in action and in bearing suffering.

After making clear that all of us are called to be witnesses and agents in the New Evangelization, the synod then highlighted the importance of the various members of the Church in the work of the New Evangelization. Bishops and priests, along with deacons, were identified as "the decisive leadership core of the New Evangelization" (Prop. 49: Pastoral Dimension of the Ordained Ministry). The synod also highlighted the fact that those in consecrated life "will offer a significant contribution to the New Evangelization" (Prop. 50: Consecrated Life).

The central role of the lay faithful was also of great importance for the New Evangelization according to the synod. The synod wrote, "The laity cooperate in the Church's work of evangelization, as witnesses and at the same time as living instruments they share in her saving mission (cf. *Ad gentes*, 41)" (Prop. 45: The Role of the Lay Faithful in the New Evangelization).

The synod also identified the family as an important agent in the New Evangelization. Proposition 48 says, "Established by the Sacrament of Matrimony, the Christian family as the domestic Church is the locus and first agent in the giving of life and love, the transmission of faith, and the formation of the human person according to the values of the Gospel" (Prop. 48: The Christian Family). Finally, the synod did not forget to underline the importance of the youth as protagonists in the New Evangelization. The synod wrote that the youth "are not only the recipients but also agents of evangelization, especially with their peers" (Prop. 51: Youth and the New Evangelization).

Each of these groups, which merits recognition in a specific proposition, deserves special consideration as efforts go forward to enliven the Church in the renewal of faith and spiritual life which is at the heart of the New Evangelization.

QUALITIES OF THE NEW EVANGELIZERS

In concluding this reflection, I want to note some of the qualities required for the new evangelizer today. There are many that can be identified, but four stand out: boldness or courage, connectedness to the Church, a sense of urgency, and joy.

In the Acts of the Apostles, the word that describes the apostles after the outpouring of the Holy Spirit at Pentecost is "bold." Peter is depicted as boldly standing up and preaching the Good News of the Resurrection, and later Paul takes up the theme and in frenetic movement around the world accessible to him, he boldly announces the Word.

Today, the New Evangelization must show a *boldness* born of confidence in Christ. Examples abound of a quiet boldness: Saint Maximilian Kolbe, Blessed Teresa of Calcutta, and before them Blessed Miguel Pro as well as the recent martyrs of Lithuania, Spain, Mexico, and the more distant witness by the saints of Korea, Nigeria, and Japan.

The evangelizers for the New Evangelization need also a *connectedness* with the Church, her Gospel, and her pastoral presence. The authentication of what we proclaim and the verification of the truth of our message is vital. We must show how these are the words of everlasting life. We must witness to our communion with the Church and our solidarity with its pastors.

Another quality of the New Evangelization and, therefore, those engaged in it is a *sense of urgency*. Perhaps we need to see in Luke's account of Mary's visitation of Elizabeth a model for our own sense of urgency. The Gospel recounts how Mary set off in haste in a long and difficult journey from Nazareth to a hill country in the village of Judea. There was no time to be lost because her mission was so important.

Finally, when we look around and see the vast field open, waiting for us to sow seeds of new life, we must do so with *joy*. In one of the final presentations of the synod, a woman from Africa, one of the auditors at the synod, reminded all of us to smile when we teach the Good News. She added, "Even bishops can smile."

Our message should be one that inspires others joyfully to follow us along the path to the kingdom of God. Joy must characterize the evangelizer. Ours is a message of great joy: Christ is risen, Christ is with us. Whatever our circumstances, our witness should radiate with the fruits of the Holy Spirit, including love, peace, and joy (cf. Gal 5:22).

Sharing the Faith

Into our world we need to communicate our own joy of being definitively and completely loved by Christ and, therefore, capable of loving others. Our communication should be in words and in life, in prayer and in deed, in action and in bearing suffering.

SUMMARY

The New Evangelization calls "all believers to renew their faith, and in their personal encounter with Jesus Christ in the Church to deepen their appreciation of the truth of the faith and joyfully to share it." As we participate in the New Evangelization, we are encouraged to be bold in our confidence in Christ, connected to the Church, infused with a sense of urgency, and filled with everlasting joy.

FOR REFLECTION

How might we be the face of Christ for those around us? What are some ways to infuse our daily lives with the joy of the Good News? What are some ways you join in the building of the God's kingdom here on earth?

CONCLUSION

"You Will Be My Witnesses" (Acts 1:8)

In answer to the question, why the New Evangelization now? I think we can say with assurance that there is an awakening of the Spirit in the hearts of many people, young and not so young, that the pretentions of the secular order are not able to satisfy the longings of the human heart. We can profess with pride and conviction that the Gospel message continues to be the answer to our needs and the longings of today. We re-propose Christ as the answer to a world staggering under the weight of so many unanswered questions of the heart.

At the very core, however, of our conviction is our faith. We proclaim this faith with renewed adherence, awakened conviction, and great joy: Christ has died, Christ is risen, and Christ will come again.

For the first disciples who encountered the Risen Christ, life was never the same. The same is true for us, as Jesus's disciples in today's world. As agents of the New Evangelization, we are called to renew and deepen our faith, grow in confidence in its truth, and joyfully share it with others. Renewed by the Eucharist, by daily prayer, and by the Sacrament of Penance, we can proclaim the Good News that Jesus Christ is risen and is with us.

Jesus gave those first disciples the Great Commission to bring his Gospel to the ends of the earth. That commission is now ours. We must share our faith, and the opportunities are everywhere. By our words and by the witness of our lives, we can proclaim Jesus's Good News to those who may have drifted away from the faith or never heard the Gospel. This sharing can be with family members across the dinner table, with our next-door neighbors, with colleagues at work, even at the sidelines at children's soccer games. Standing in the truth of our faith, we can share that truth with love.

Today, like the first disciples, we can be Jesus's witnesses, and proclaim his Good News in our everyday lives. With our hearts transformed by Christ, we can change the hearts of others, and transform the world.

As the bishops emphasized at the Synod for the New Evangelization, this is a new moment in the life of the Church, a new Pentecost. It's our turn now to share the great gift we have been given, the gift of our Catholic faith, and renew the face of the earth.

ABOUT THE AUTHOR

CARDINAL DONALD WUERL is the archbishop of Washington, the author of numerous books and articles, and was recently the general relator (moderator) at the Synod of Bishops on the New Evangelization for the Transmission of the Christian Faith.